A Porn Star Love Life

You make me blush my dear.
~Steve Holmes

A PORN STAR LOVE LIFE

2015 - 2019

ISBN 978-1-716-27727-6

available at lulu.com
written under pseudonym LS Harteveld
cover photo Katrina Cooper-Hinton
somerandomchick.picfair.com

www.lsharteveld.nl
Twitter @LSHarteveld

There are two ways to reach me:
by way of kisses or by way of the imagination.

But there is a hierarchy: the kisses alone don't work.

~ Anais Nin

1
50 SHADES OF STOYA

There are definitely benefits to a blogging sabbatical.
And the moment you add a 7 week long Twitter fasting, for full commitment, you get to watch even more interesting phenomena.

First of all, the moment I stopped writing for the LS Harteveld site, I immediately launched a super labor intensive project on my yoga blog. This is my professional blog where I am an average garden variety yoga teacher.
Apparently I needed something to do, and was eager to fill in the void (and not with working on my books).

The yoga writing project started out pretty neutral (how to develop your personal practice, that sort of thing) but soon I was sharing everything, burdening my students with my love life and the capacity to write in 50 funky anecdotes to spice up one topic, which was usually only vaguely related to yoga in the first place.

Since I was still keeping in touch with all my deviant/ more interesting friends through Twitter, I decided to close down that account for 7 weeks.
I really expected something close to a miracle...

That I would live in this ocean of peace, a social media low heaven, where I would be a serenely smiling yoga teacher by day, and a serenely smiling secretive diarist working on her book. Also by day. At night I would get 8.5 hours of sleep.

Yet what happened?

I opened a Twitter account for my work.

Uh oh.

And I became GOOD.

I made new friends, who felt drawn to me because I was a yoga teacher, or someone who lived around the corner, or because we liked the same wine bar. I hooked up with other local entrepreneurs and I acquired a new level of being part of my local community.

And a new level of being an internet addict.

Just with new friends, and a new blog to write for.

Uh oh.

But there is still stuff I can't share with them. And that part of me, the kinky side, the provocative one, the slightly aggressive one (oh, a little harder than that), the gruesomely submissive ..... that all, has no place to go.

So thank God for this newsletter!!

And by now I'm sure you're thinking: Who's Stoya? Make your point you crazy woman!

Okay: Stoya is a girl crush, just like escort Avery Moore.

I was actively idolizing Avery, a pale, toned, 1000 dollars an hour escort-who-could-also-write-really-well, but Avery was a difficult love to feed because she didn't show her face on pictures, only her voice on interviews, and she recently sealed off her site so that visitors now have to create an account first.

But the Huffington Post gave me something better than Avery: Stoya!

The article was called: "Can A Porn Star Be America's Sweetheart?" (Of course!!)

And Stoya turned out to be a pale, toned, porn star-who-could-also-write-really-well, but who showed her lovely Snow White face absolutely everywhere!

If it wasn't for their breasts – Avery is full bosomed, and Stoya is a striking cup B but only if she feeds on ice cream for a week (her words) – I wouldn't be able to tell them apart.

And after a few weeks of drooling over Stoya I realized she is the missing ingredient from the Hollywood movie 50 Shades of Grey. I think anyone who has seen it will agree it would have been much better as a high budget porn, showing in theatres (probably the first main stream porn since Emmanuelle!) all over the world.

And Stoya looks more innocent than Dakota Johnson (the current actress), her sex scenes would do the book justice, and she would definitely know how to appreciate a good spanking.

Just like me.

50 Shades of Stoya
was written on 17 March 2015

2
PORN KING

Every time someone asks me how my summer is going, I answer: "I'm not going anywhere".
No days off or weeks on holiday.
And yet, I have this feeling I'm overlooking something, because I feel as if I just got back from a 7 week surfing holiday in the Bay of Biscay.

I clearly must be overlooking something...

And then it hit me!
Of course!
I've started on my sexual bucket list with Mr.Big and his performance proved to be above any expectations.

"You're now dating a porn king," a friend said.

It was a compliment that at the same time indicated I shouldn't be making any plans. Porn kings are not relationship material. Yet the thought rooted in my brain, and developed a whole new line of thinking.

First, let me admit I made a mistake, dropped the ball, neglected my defenses, that sort of thing:

I told Mr.Big I'm in love with him, and that I would make him mine the moment he leaves his wife.

Uh oh. That's two things you should not do if you want a chance at winning or even surviving dating a player: To show your weak spots AND share your strategy.

But I did mean it.

The sexual bucket list hardly ever came to table with the other men, in the eight years I had been dating. I had started to believe that garden variety sex was all there was.

I used to have so much more potential and Mr.Big reminded me of that.

And to then think that in the beginning I resisted him!

I refused to answer The Call of him and me becoming lovers.

I remember a conversation, very vividly, where I told Biggie I would not date him because he was a "Major League player", and would break my heart, and so on.

Until I went home and thought;

"Wait a minute!! I have devoted 8 years to my love life and sex life. And then I finally meet a worthy opponent and I say boo hoo hoo, you'll break my heart?

Then for what have I been training?

If I'm not ready to date in the Major League, then which woman is? I can't possibly let a 20 year old take my place!"

So I went back in, faced Mr. Big, and said:
"Bring. It. On."
And he did.
And a few months later, we were doing things from my bucket list.

Sure I wanted him to be my man; Who wouldn't want to put a ring on that?

And then someone said: "You're dating a porn king,"
Followed by: "You're his equal. If you want, he'll keep you on as a mistress, regardless of his other relationships."
And: not to underestimate the power of the forbidden. That our affair had the potential to last a lifetime.

And I had never thought of it that way.

I had always approached it as a game, where the last woman standing would win. And me admitting my feelings to him, was not well played, but that our affair could result in a life long tie?
I had never considered that.

For days, I kept thinking about it. How were we playing this game? What were my advantages, and my weaknesses?

I reconsidered the role of his wife.

I had always seen her as my opponent, but now I saw it was a lot more complicated than that. That her presence was actually working for me, not against me. She was keeping him cornered. Sure, Mr.Big could still move around, and enough to fit in a secret mistress.

But nevertheless, his range of motion would be far greater, if he didn't have his family to attend to.

If she was taken out of the game, he would be set free, and there was no telling for which team he would be playing or in which hoop he would score.

And I wondered what I wanted out of this?

Contrary to Mr.Big I am extremely good with relationships. They're harmonious, cozy, fun. And this goes for all my relationships. I have excellent credentials.

Yet what I want out of this, more than anything, and what Mr.Big is offering me where all the others failed, is a sexual partner in crime to work down that bucket list with.
To make up new things.

Of course I would love to really get to know Mr.Big, but I have a far better shot at getting what I want (great sex) if I leave the whole relationship theme out of it.

Porn King.

You're his equal.

Seeing a relationship with Big as impossible, or him as too difficult, is just as chicken as backing out to date him. I am his sexual equal and have that impressive rep sheet of 100% harmonious relationships. If I'm not ready to have a relationship with him, then who is?

I'm in it to win it. I'm gonna work the whole field, score in the right hoop, and if the court is cleared, and the new match starts, I won't retreat but step up and say:

Bring. It. On.

Porn King
was written on 8 August 2015

3
AND AWAY IS AVERY.
HOW A DISAPPEARING ESCORT BECAME MY MUSE

Early 2014 there was a $1000 an hour escort named Avery Moore, who had time tracked an entire year in business. How much time she spent with company, how many shoes she got, the number of dinners or books received.

And I was totally intrigued.

Because not only did I turn out to have a dormant obsession for pale, petite sex workers (which I later projected onto porn star Stoya), but I'm a diligent planner and time tracker myself.

I even bought my first and only leather Filofax agenda in 1991 living on a student allowance because I watched a detective where the escort (murdered, unfortunately) had possessed a similar luxurious agenda. With her name on it. It sparked my love for sex workers, and made getting a similar agenda a priority. In 2014, Avery Moore was the first since 1991 to hit these two kinks again – sex and stationary. Although Avery Moore used software mostly, but close enough.

Avery Moore became my time management crush.

I do have a major disappointment coming up for you, but before we get there let's first remember the good times. Because in those days, she had a website. It contained her rates, sassy "me" and "you" pages, and gorgeous photos that would seduce you so thoroughly, you practically threw your credit card at the screen. She also kept a blog. And she could write. She wrote well.

It was so good this journalist gave up any idea of doing a better job himself, and just quoted half her blog, admitting "I'm cribbing phrases of this woman."

Halfway 2015 Avery disappeared. Her website Away with Avery dot com was first password protected, until eventually it was bought or claimed by one of those eerie companies that prey on the remains of once successful websites. Like vultures on dead beasts.

A dreadful ending.

I still wonder whatever happened to her. Did she get pregnant? Retired?

On her late website, as well as in this radio interview, the only available recording of her and one of the very few traces she has ever existed, she makes the impression that she really loved her job.
Just like me, she was young when she learned what escorts were, and she looked up to them thinking;
"No... that can't be me. That's way too high up!"

I personally never tried my luck, but she did, and she loved her job. Then why did she leave? When her career was just about to take off and she could have taken her brand anywhere she wanted?

There are moments when I browse through the videos of female business coaches and I just know Avery could have become an author, motivational speaker or first class VIP business coach. Her classy, clear, alluring website was proof of that.

Why didn't she use the momentum she had?

But I'm grateful our virtual paths crossed, during that short time window when she made media appearances. I was inspired by her presence then, and every time my life needs a make-over I make a list of new habits and challenges and stuff I want to do daily in order to live a successful life, and I sum it up as one thing;

Become Avery Moore.

I hope that wherever she is, and whatever she's doing, that she still has the same zest for life, and still inspires the people around her, touching their heart and soul, or perhaps a little lower.

And that she still asks a thousand dollars an hour.

Because I know for a fact she's worth every penny.

And AWAY Is Avery. How a disappearing escort became my muse was written on 12 April 2017

4
WHY MY NAKED ASS IS NOT IN A MAGAZINE TODAY

I just attended my first birthday party in years. Because for what seemed like a decade – or wait! it *was* a decade! – my writing came first. Writing was my work addiction, my leisure activity, my personal development tool, and my preferred company to spend my nights alone with. If someone wanted a shot at me getting away from my computer I only did so for two reasons.

1. I really liked their company

or

2. I really liked their company and we were going to have sex

I never invested time in meeting new people, and I didn't engage in group activities with unsorted social interaction.
Spending time away from my writing only served as a way to get a fresh pair of eyes on the matter at hand (or "pen") through conversation with others, or to do activities that I knew would inspire a new diary entry or erotic story.

Inspiration or analysis.
Those were the only two needs I had aside from writing. Randomly getting to know new people or spending nights away without a clear purpose, was not on the menu.

The party however, was everything I hoped for. I must admit I was invited by someone who knew "presence" and "leveling" were not in my repertoire, and that the only way to have me, was to have ALL of me.

I was going to be my bold, entertaining, provocative self.

Halfway through the evening I had gathered a small crowd of people who had gotten me talking about my single years. Which included bedding multiple men half my age, a Mossad spy, a broad selection of men of exotic descent, and a married man, Mister Big.

I knew Mister Big was a keeper when he gave me my first time anal sex. A flawless performance. After eight years of diverse material, and various disappointments, I immediately recognized a star player. With the others I had turned a blind eye on almost everything, before we finally got down and dirty (and I knew I could take it from there!) Whereas with Mister Big I only had to condone that he was married and that the matter was never ever to be discussed other than a vague "It's complicated".

A fair price to pay, for the performance he was able to give. So I paid. I never asked for more. And we're heading for our three year unsolicited sex anniversary, so worth the investment.

I was explaining to my crowd exactly how brittle female sexuality is. A guy can screw it up by not being attentive enough, or by being too pushy. He can throw away his chances by the heating not being on, when you enter his house at night. Or by sleeping with the windows open.

I have a theory!

And this is such a good story that it is worth a separate blogpost but I'm just going to throw it in now. The theory is – and I'm almost a hundred percent sure I'm right! – the theory is that the special breed of men who know exactly what a woman wants, and who are even more in tune with her desires, quirks and pains than she is herself, that the few men who are the womanizers that are able to read women, just like a horse whisperer can read horses, that those men have one thing in common; They had a dominant mother, and they pleased her.

They fought her too, don't get me wrong.

But it was never with the intention of changing their relationship to one that was based on being equal. He fought her as a way to stay into contact, and he was never mean to her. Even though she? Yes...she could be mean, although he would never call it that.

She was jealous of his girlfriends, and fought it with arguments like him needing to do his homework.

Or with the girl not being good enough.

She was often disappointed by the countless ways in which he didn't live up to her expectations. And he internalized it. He too became disappointed with himself, and he was especially sorry for not being able to please her.

But he stayed. And he could read his mother.

Just a twitch in her voice, or an answer that took a bit too long, and he would know he had displeased her. And sometimes he growled, but he knew what to do. Maybe he went away giving her time to cool off. Until, like all women obsessed with a man, she had driven herself crazy with her thoughts and she became hysterical for his attention.

Or maybe he did have some sort of friendly method to calm her down.

But whatever it was? It molded him. Where other men learned to adjust a carburetor just from listening closely, this particular type of man with a dominant mother coped by paying meticulous attention to what his mother needed.

And his first girlfriends, who he immediately knew better than they knew themselves especially at that young age, got hooked on him. It was inevitable.

They felt safe, and loved.

And the boy noticed his friends were being way better with cars than with girls, and he tried to inform them that really- women weren't that difficult. You just had to listen carefully.

But even with prospect of having any girl fall for them, and being able to fulfill any of their most pornographic fantasies with the girl willingly agreeing, even that prospect couldn't motivate them to listen to the advice from the boy with the dominant mother.

And the boy became a man whose bedroom and house were always comfortably warm, he became a partner who knew exactly what you wanted to hear and a lover who knew precisely what to do to turn you on and take you next level.

I told this theory to my audience, and asked them if they believed my theory was right, and the first thing someone said was:
"Those men don't exist!"

Oh, but they do...

Because crucial in my storytelling was the first night I went home with Mister Big. I didn't want sex. We had kissed a while back, and that was nice but not earth shattering.

I had decided I would make out with him every once in a while, but had no intention of becoming a secret mistress. I had judged being a mistress somewhere between being seedy and being emotionally dangerous. I wasn't in love with him (or so I thought) and the kissing at a bar had been okay, but it had not set me on fire head to toe, so it all seemed okay.

I was sure I could contain it.

Mister Big was exciting and he oozed danger, but I knew he would never want to do anything against my will.

If anything, he would manipulate me until I was begging for it.

But with the kissing being down-to-earth and nice, I was sure I could safely go to his house for some TLC without being either raped or swept away by desire.

Or so I thought. Suffice to say I only just managed to get away unfucked. But it all started almost coolly, and in a way any normal man would have almost certainly fucked up.

We entered his apartment.

The hallway was nice and warm.

And suddenly, I felt super conscious of the situation. I was alone, with someone I had known for only a few weeks, and no one knew where I was. I got slightly nervous. Mister Big didn't seem to notice. He rooted a bit around the house in a casual fashion. As if it was the most common thing in the world to bring blonde erotica writers into your house in the middle of the night.

"And you know what he did?" I asked my audience.

Which now included a ten month old baby who had the talent to laugh or drop his jaw at exactly the right moment. The baby shook his head.

"He took his shoes off and asked if I wanted a cup of tea."

The female audience was now screaming and yelling:
"No!"

"Brilliant!"

"He's good!"

But one man couldn't see how offering tea was a good idea when you've just managed to get an attractive woman passing through your door. So for him I needed to explain what just happened. And what made Mister Big so good.

Where normal men are way too preoccupied with their own insecurities, and desires, on moments such as these, Mister Big – and other highly talented womanizers – stay in touch with the woman. They are so sensitive to a woman's need, that they know exactly what is required. In this case, Mister Big had sensed I was intimidated and he totally downplayed himself. Exactly the way a horse whisperer has to pretend he's not interested in the horse, and will keep his distance where the horse can come closer on its own accord. In the same way, Mister Big pretended he had no particular interest in me being there. Least of all getting into my panties.

I elaborated on my affair with Mister Big, and how the years together had given me powerful insights into my own sexuality and personality. And that I now fully identify with being a secret mistress. If this relationship would end, I would choose to be someone else's secret mistress.

It was late. I had talked for an hour or maybe even more. And yet both me, and the other people there, seemed to have a desire for more. Like a little dessert.

"Can I show them what's in the bag?" I asked my friend who was having her birthday. "You already know, and I've been dying to show it. But I want to know if it's okay."

The friend said it was okay, and reminded me I had been invited with the promise that I could totally be myself.

I took a glossy magazine from my bag, and showed it to them.

"Today is an incredible festive today. Because in this magazine, you will not find my naked ass. Even though I was invited to be in it."

The magazine changed hands quickly, and we paid special attention to the ten pages that had all the women who had said "yes" to the invitation. I wondered if they had always thought getting butt naked in a magazine was a good idea, or if it was something they had done because they had a sort of "try everything once" philosophy to life.

All I knew for certain was that I was happy that Mister Big had never tried to get me out of my panties to pose butt naked in a magazine. Because he would have played his cards so well, that I would have ended up fucking begging for it.

Why my naked ass is not in a magazine today
was written on 10 September 2017

5
A, MY, BRIEF HISTORY OF SEX

I have been fascinated with sex for as long as I can remember. I played doctor from when I was 5, 6 years old. A sex game I happily picked up as an adult.

And when I was in my early teens and my father got rid of his collection of nude magazines, I quickly curated them from the paper recycle bin. I loved going through those glossy pages that so openly discussed what already fascinated me most in life, even though I barely had my first period;
Sex

Together with the nude models came Xaviera Hollander, who had a column in Penthouse, with a penis shaped lipstick. I didn't understand the meaning of the shape, or the image. But I liked it either way, and spelled out her columns.
I think Xaviera's page was Q&A, but I can't remember.

Nor do I know when (or why!!) I eventually got rid of the stack of magazines, especially because I didn't buy new ones.
They were all I had until I got a boyfriend who was as open about owning them as my father had been.
Despite the promising start, I almost never came into contact with the sex industry, nor did I watch or own pornography.

I visited the Sex Museum in Amsterdam last weekend.
It was founded in 1985 by a woman who was 20 at the time. Her father had owned an arcade at a premium location; right at the route every train passenger and tourist walks.

But the arcade had to shut down because of a rise in crime, and that's when his daughter stepped in.

She bought an eclectic collection of sex magazines, toys, and paraphernalia. She later referred to it as "rubbish" but part of her original collection maintains to this day!
Just check out the back; a small dark room, where you can see about twenty large frames with cut and paste crafting work featuring anal sex, fisting, BDSM – all dating from 1985.

I like that they kept that little touch of nostalgia – of the humble beginnings – even though the museum is much bigger now, and the young owner all grown up.

I met her at an antiquarian book auction in the nineties.
I was bidding for my father, and she was the only other woman there. She was beautifully dressed, and very friendly to me. I'll never forgot the excitement when she told me who she was, and what she was buying there.

Maybe we also connected because we were both daddy's girls, I don't know.

Either way, what I meant to say by not having a lot to do with the sex industry, was that contrary to for example that intriguing woman who had founded the sex museum, I had a boring career and love life too. I became an academic, just like my father. I had long term relationships. No one cheated. It was absolutely boring.

I know what kept me from pursuing what I really wanted – or even what kept me from finding out what it was I wanted. So I can forgive myself. Because it takes a lot of nerve and strength to figure out your sexuality, and I didn't have that as a teen, nor did I have it in my twenties.

But I did know I wasn't interested in sex the way others were; as relationship glue.

I found sex with the secondary interest of establishing or maintaining a shared life outside the bedroom, severely limiting.
It's like saying; "Let's see who can jump the furthest," facing a brick wall at 2 meters.

For a long time I thought my faithfulness was fake and that deep down I wanted other partners. That it was monogamy that was killing my lust. That's what you get if you don't figure things out; you assume.

But in hindsight I didn't mind having sex with the same person.
I just disliked having a relationship with him at the same time. This epiphany took me ten years of being single to figure out. So that's a long time.
But yes, I am monogamous.
I call it; My kink.
Things get more exciting for me, if I can focus on one man, and one man only.

Having more of them, would be hugely straining. I dread the day I am in love with two men, and they would both want to date me.
I would have to step up my game, get out of my comfort zone of monogamy, and love them both.

But outside of the relationship component- there was a second reason my previous monogamous "affairs" aka long term relationships never worked;
Because I desire a man to be non-monogamous.
Maybe that's evidence of the sexually rich and exciting start I had.

But I get bored at the idea of him being devoted to me, and not wanting to bother go chase other women.
It's not that I need to know the specifics, or that I want to be part of a threesome (maybe I could- I don't know).
I just want him to totally own his sexuality and his autonomy.

If I would ask him about other women, I would want him hug me close and answer;
"That excites you, doesn't it?"

It may look like a docile ending, with me all monogamous even though I was into sex at such an early age.

But ultimately what it comes down to, is that I simply refuse to settle for any man who doesn't arouse me, surprise me, and lure me in with the same seductive power as that stack of nude magazines had on a thirteen year old girl.

A, my, Brief History of Sex
was written on 26 October 2017

6
50 SHADES OF MAY THIS LAST FOREVER

On the fourth day of my project of living planning-free, and basically doing whatever the fuck I want to, I accidentally discovered the upside of NOT being able to do what you want to do: Abstinence, not doing your soul's work, does heighten the sensations of pleasure after.

Because before I had this day going, before I had dived into all the stuff I felt like doing, the ball got rolling on something that I had been wanting to do for a long time. But this morning I got a cue that I had to do it immediately.

No time to lose.

The cue was that a writer about whom I had written a book four years ago, was publishing his second novel today. And this meant that today was the ideal day to reblog the diary he had inspired; to publish it online.

I've published ten books and my ultimate goal is to have them all online, for free. So then either you could read them for free on my website, or buy a paper copy. No pdf's or e-reader stuff.

I'm sure that's not the choice most authors would make, but that's my choice. It's the way I have envisioned it, and that's what's going to happen.

Except that nothing was happening because reblogging stuff is pain in the ass work I don't want to do. Not unless of course there is this HUGE incentive of a book suddenly becoming current again. Like today.

So I knew I wanted to reblog the book, and I did.

Which cost me four hours, instead of the ninety minutes I had estimated.

By the time I finished it I was terribly hungry because I had skipped my lunch and was way past my feeding time. But on a soul level, I also felt unfulfilled. Thirsty. Desperate for anything that could take away feeling this unaccomplished.

So maybe it was because of my deprived state, that I shamelessly clicked on two tweets in my Twitter timeline that were both blatantly my kind of kink.

First I clicked Steve Holmes' retweet of a movie called Darker Side of Desire

Steve Holmes is a porn actor who I know from a video of him and Stoya in Paris. That is a series that Stoya shoots herself, taking the camera with her all over the world. I was a paying member of TrenchcoatX, and watched all of them. Until I realized that the one I kept coming back to, was the one in Paris, with Steve Holmes.

Where beautiful young Stoya (my favorite porn actress) hit it off with this middle aged man I didn't know... yet. And I also couldn't quite figure out why I liked that video so much.

Until I looked him up.

It turned out the Actor Steve Holmes was also the Director and Producer Steve Holmes. And now I saw it... yes.

Steve Holmes had "directed" this video, by operating the camera. He had been the one who had filmed the close-up shots that I had liked so much. Stoya's other videos were more filmed from afar, with the camera on a stand, or sometimes held by Stoya.

But Steve had a better view while filming, plus decades of experience. No wonder that video of him and Stoya totally rocked.

Anyway, that's how I know Steve and I started following him on Twitter, and he posts or retweets trailers of movies he has worked on. They're always really kinky and I totally love them.

This one, Darker Side of Desire, was more high budget and with a real story line. It was about a young woman whose relationship with her dominant had ended, and she missed having a dominant so much. Suddenly I realized that if my lover Mr.Big and me would end, I would feel the same way.

That the breakup would mean so much more than "just" losing the man I love.

It would also mean losing the only man who knows exactly what makes me tick. I don't see myself succeeding at dating "vanilla" style, any more than the girl in the movie did.

And with Mr.Big and me, it's not even that we would count as being into BDSM. But our preferred roles, of him being dominant and me submissive, are fixed. And I know that's hard to come by.

The second tweet I clicked was a piece of Girl on the Net about Being Lazy in Bed, in which I immediately recognized my preference for being submissive and still.

Girl on the Net is the only woman when it comes to sharing kinks, who I can relate to. All women who write about their sexual journey, make me realize that my sexual preference is surprisingly narrow. With no need for leather, whips, or sex dungeons. Nor for tantra, massage or valley orgasms.

I want it exactly the way I want it, and nothing else.

I remember a conversation with a friend a little while back, where I confessed that I had never been very interested in the physical part of sex.
"I like the mental part, you know?" I explained. "Where you dive into the depths of your mind, and tell each other stuff you don't dare tell a soul."
She immediately replied: "Yes, you mean perverted."
Exactly.

Whenever I hear good sex in relationships is about intimacy and connecting, I always think: "Yes. And No."
Because intimacy is only arousing, after you first had a fight of some sorts.
Honesty is refreshing, when it comes from someone who usually lies. And trust is only an aphrodisiac if there is also something you're scared of.

You can't have the yin without the yang.

But to have your sex life rooted in shared sexual fantasies?
That's amazing.

It's a win-win, never a dull moment kind of relationship. And it's also very rare, unfortunately. It's that aspect, of two perfectly matching sexual preferences, that I would miss the most.

We've been together for way over three years, yet I feel there's still so much to discover. We barely got a taste of everything we're capable of. Maybe because we're apart 99% of the time, with him not necessary lying to me but definitely unavailable 99% of the time.
It makes the 1% we're together intoxicating and delicious.

Reading the article from Girl on the Net on being lazy or submissive, and watching the trailer of the movie about the young female submissive, made me realize that my relationship with Big has amplified my sexual preference.

That the submissive part, the fixed role playing part, the carte blanche I'm getting to share whatever deviant desire I have, and to then have someone who is eager to play it out, and to fully dominate me.
It has become who I am.
This, being submissive in bed, has become non-negotiable.

And if I ever, God forbid, become single again – technically I'm still single of course, since I'm a secret mistress I don't have a status – that I will start dating new men not only based on who I like.
But also on who wants to play.

The trailer of the porn movie ends with the young woman interviewing a dominant (Steve Holmes) for her thesis. He answers the questions but then interrupts her: "You're not here to ask me questions." She replies that she's no longer into that sort of thing.

He offers her a gift, a little box with a small insertable toy, with which he can control her.
"Give me twenty-four hours to change your mind."

I would say Yes.

50 Shades of May This Last Forever
was written on 2 May 2018

7
TREATING MYSELF TO
A NEW BODY FOR MY BIRTHDAY

For a while now, I've been moderately obsessed with getting my old body back. And I've restarted this challenge at least once a week and often even had the audacity to publicly announce my physical transformation.

Only to then never speak of it again when I dropped off the wagon of doing more yoga and working less.
And instead didn't do any yoga and worked even harder than ever before.
So I never got "there".

Just yesterday, within days after cutting a deal with myself that these blog posts were going to be written in an hour, so that I had a chance of taking care of my basic physical needs with yoga, home cooked meals, daylight and a bike ride;
I turned myself inside out at my writing desk and came up with a piece that stretched three hours and three decades.
Bye bye basic needs.

I did have a bike ride though, because I always clean the yoga studio on Tuesdays. So then the bike ride is work, which means there is a hundred percent higher chance that I'll actually prioritize it.

So I was in the city, and my day had went awol first because of the way too long blogpost and then by a draining but effective series of phone calls and paperwork for last week's credit card fraud.

I was now walking the streets with an envelop, which I could not post anywhere because postal services have removed half of their mailboxes. To keep my spirits up, I was eating a double scoop of Belgian cream.

That's when I "ran" (I could not have been strolling slower, honestly. Looking around halfheartedly for mailboxes) into Disciplined Friend. Like all Disciplined Friends I have, he has an irrepressible urge to downplay his own achievements and to remind you of how many times he slacked and didn't run, lift weights, or do yoga. Depending on which disciplined friend it is.

Disciplined Friend was in his running gear, and he was cooling down. So we had a little chat.

I confessed to him that whenever he posted his run on Facebook, it inspired me.
From what I hear that is an atypical response to workout updates.
There's even a meme:
"Unless you find a dead body on your morning run, I don't want to know about it."
But I like knowing you worked out.

I told him that I sometimes wished he would text me, to announce that he would go running. It would be crucial that he did this before he went, not after.

And then I would pause writing my lengthy blog posts, postpone calling credit card companies, and do an amazing one hour super-intensive yoga session, that totally transformed my body and my life. And I would do that three to four times a week.
And it would be *amaaaayzing*.

"And then of course I think: There's an app for that," I concluded my story.

I quickly started licking my ice cream all the way around because it was really hot and I couldn't afford having a conversation.

I saw the letter in my hand already contained ice cream stains as well.

We said our goodbyes, I found a mailbox, cleaned my studio, taught my classes, and sat myself down for my last hour of the day, which is sacred time. I clear out my running diary, go through all the notes of that day, transfer them to my diary or notebooks and cross off all the pages that don't contain relevant information anymore.

I could see where I had "lost" my resolution to do yoga: on days when I already have six hours of designated work, I can't afford writing a three hour blog post and then expect to do an hour of yoga as well.

But also; the eating.

It's not that I can't have an ice cream, but I knew I was slipping back into my habit of needing food in order to make myself keep up with everything I have to do. I use food as fuel. Whereas when I'm writing? Journaling? Taking a personal development training?

Then I can go up to seven hours without needing food, water or Wifi.

So Monday and Tuesday are my most challenging days in terms of self-care but they also set me up for the rest of the week. If I don't do yoga then, I don't do it the rest of the week either.

Same goes for snacking.

If I drop my "diet" of three times a day all you can eat, in favor of Belgian ice cream on Tuesday afternoons, I will easily slip into eating whatever crosses my path, twenty-four seven.

And I thought of my ideal body, my ideal lifestyle, and that every year for the last decade I had slipped away further. I have a photo in bikini top and jeans, from my 40th birthday. I vividly remember having it taken and thinking:

"Hmmm... I can't believe I still fit into these pants. I'm way heavier than I want to be. But my belly looks nice. I hope this photo inspires me to take the extra pounds off."

That was five years and eight kilos ago.

And then, like a lightning rod, it struck me. A powerful vision of exactly the way I want my body to be.

Lean.

Bendy.

Professional.

It was as if my two ideal bodies, those of porn star Stoya and of escort Avery Moore mixed together with a new vision of Who I Wanted To Be, the second half of my life.

What was different from all the resolutions I had before, was that I no longer felt resistant to work for it. For the first time in my life I saw my body as a commodity, something that could pay the bills.

Which isn't even that far off considering I am a yoga teacher, and the only offers I have gotten as a writer is to pose half nude or fully nude. In "exchange for free publicity".

I don't know why I put quotation marks there, since it means exactly what it says. I said no, or hell no, or fuck no, but I do acknowledge that a writer with a killer body is definitely more newsworthy than a middle aged woman struggling to keep the pounds off.

It was clear to me that my decision to commit to this daily blog, and thereby a decision to get serious with my writing, could only be followed by a decision to be just that driven in getting the sex worker body to match it.

I wonder if there's an app for that.

Treating myself to a new body for my birthday was written on 9 May 2018

8
A PORN STAR LOVE LIFE

My love for porn started with Stoya.

But after watching every interview with her, and reading all her newsletters, yet still only sporadically watching her movies, I realized that it had little to do with porn.

And that the only thing that had started with my love for Stoya, was my love for Stoya.

Then I thought I had really fallen for porn again, after seeing Steve Holmes.

Until of course I realized that the only thing I had fallen for, was Steve Holmes.

Steve is more often than not cast as a sadist, a dominant or some other deviant middle aged man. When on his YouTube channel, where he interviews the talent before and after their scene with him, he confesses that for him seeing a girl naked is more than enough to be happy and have a good time.

Steve Holmes is so charming and sweet with all the girls he interviews. He gives a little kiss on a naked knee, frequently apologizes that his English is not so good (Steve is German), and I just know he is the perfect man to try out all the stuff you would never dare ask a normal man.

I know we will never hear bad stories about him #metoo-ing his way through porn land. He puts every woman at ease, even when she's contractually obliged to have sex with him.

And Steve is married!

Isn't that a nice thought that this man just goes back to his wife at the end of the day. I would marry him, too. I love the idea of a man bringing in the sexual energy into a relationship!

And although I haven't shared much about my love for Stoya here: I nurture similar sympathetic feelings for her. Although less sexual, because I'm straight. But Stoya could be my best friend, and we would talk cats, because she has the sweetest cat in the world.
His name is Pixel because he only has one eye.
And Stoya is a writer too.

So, despite me always thinking I'm going after the porn, and am motivated by my twisted preferences, in the end I immediately forget about all of that and get stuck in the tenderness and cuteness of it all. I'm sure this does explain why I need a man to bring in the sexual energy.
Because I drop that ball at the sight of the first one-eyed-cat.

Yesterday I went to see friends and they made me dinner. And I talked about Steve Holmes and how good he was with women. And somehow, in that same conversation, I had the most amazing revelation.
It was an interesting perspective.
I am currently in a secret relationship with a married man. We've been "together" (we see each other very little) for three and a half years. And I've always wondered what I would do if this ended.

My most recent decision was that I would not date anyone for a while because I'm focused on my business at the moment. But after that I would create the exact same thing: I would sign up for the dating site Second Love, and become a mistress to another married man.
But somehow praising Steve Holmes sparked a new idea:
to start working in porn, instead of getting a new relationship.

I can't tell you how happy that thought made me.

Every good habit around keeping my body in mint condition, and every resolution about losing weight and doing yoga daily, immediately fell into place.

Suddenly there was a reason to do all those things.

When last week my lover proposed a date, on a day I was fully booked and couldn't possibly make it, I realized that even if I could make it? I didn't have time for ALL the grooming I had to do in order to be the least bit fuckable.

My lover is more a Steve Holmes kind of guy: he will enjoy me naked in any shape or form.

But I need to be freshly showered, shaved and trimmed in order to feel like it.

So I did all that anyway, the day after. When I did have time. And I realized I had no reason to pay attention to my body. I wasn't having sex. And if I'm not having sex, I just lose interest in taking care of myself.

Grooming wise, but also sports or dieting.

I just can't be bothered.

So the prospect of getting a career in porn as a middle aged woman? That was a thrilling idea!

I could see myself FINALLY cleaning up my act!

And saying enough is enough!

I'm gonna lose weight, moisturize every day, trim, shave, wax, be absolutely fuckable 24/7 and live a porn star life starting NOW!

I went to bed happy and excited that I had so much good stuff waiting for me.

Naturally, I wanted to masturbate to celebrate. But I didn't really know what to fantasize about. I had masturbated to my lover Mr.Big for years, but a month or so ago, I had decided that I wasn't going to do that anymore.

That I couldn't afford to make my self-love dependent on the man who was already a liability in my real love life. If that ever ended, I needed my masturbation routine to go on, unharmed by our breakup. So that wasn't an option.
Then, much to my own surprise I must say, I suddenly thought about someone about whom I have not written in ages.

In fact, I have so dropped out of the habit of speaking about him in recent years that I don't feel like sharing his name here.
But it was someone I deeply cared for, and longed for. And of course, ultimately still do. Desire doesn't have an end date.

So I thought about being in bed with him, and making love, and although we were a bit deviant (hey! it's my fantasy, what did you expect!) it was most of all completely, utterly loving and trusting and emotional and maybe a bit heartbreaking too.
Because it had never happened in real life, and maybe it never would.

I fell asleep rethinking my resolution to go into porn if Big and I were ever over. I realized porn was not the answer. It had never been.

I had simply been drawn to it because Steve Holmes had made it look as if it was the best and most likely place, to find love.

A Porn Star Love Life
was written on 1 July 2018

9
TURNING PAIN INTO PLEASURE

Last night, when I lay awake in bed (again) and I was suffering from pain in my chest (again); I made the resolution that from this day forward, till death do me part, and I hoped me doing this was going to seriously postpone that, I was going to put self-care first.

And I was going for RADICAL self-care!
Like William Dafoe!
I would be getting up every morning, do a two hour yoga practice, and that was it.
Everything else I got done that day would be a bonus.

But despite real yogis I knew I wouldn't practice on an empty stomach, and needed breakfast and then coffee.
And I always crawled behind the computer with my coffee to write a post, which took me two to four hours.
It had usually been a blog post for the yoga studio because my focus on making money as LS Harteveld (and therefor doing daily messaging as LS Harteveld) was only a few days old.

But regardless of the account it was for (yoga studio or LSH), writing in pj's was of course not proper self-care!

So last night I got the idea to start writing the tiniest LS Harteveld sales post, while drinking my AM Latte Macchiatos.
No more lengthy blog posts.
And then I'd do the William Dafoe, and I would live happily and pain free and wildly successful ever after.

Would I just write the sales post on Facebook, and then repost it to Twitter? Or would I be missing out on sales, because people on Twitter didn't want to click a Facebook link?
And I also knew I would ultimately want to collect them!
Like a diary.

Not that I intended to publish a real book with a year of sales posts, of course not. But soon enough they would turn into really great stories that I had not told anywhere else, and then I would be uncomfortable with the idea that they were only on Facebook.

If I wanted to save myself from copy-pasting backwards through my timeline, I was better off to immediately write the sales posts in a blog, and skip the straight-into the Facebook box phase.
It was better to write them in a way they were immediately archived.

Meanwhile it was 3 AM, and I was angry that despite me having prioritized writing/ making money from LS Harteveld this week – a commitment I would keep for the rest of my life – I was still suffering the pain in my chest.
I thought that the chest pains had been caused by feeling a pressure to make money with my yoga business or as a business mentor.
Now that I had decided to focus on writing, and on selling books, I had expected the heart pains to magically disappear.

I did stop having suicidal thoughts and crying, the moment I had vetoed to never do anything with my cognitive skills or with my degree. Then why was my body still throwing pain tantrums, when there was nothing to worry about anymore?

Because this was the plan:

OPTION 1.

WRITE, SELL BOOKS, HAVE HOBBY YOGA STUDIO,
GET NEW CATS

Teaching yoga classes is the ideal leisure, to compensate for being behind my desk all day.
I was positive that when I became a famous author, I would want to have that studio to stay connected to all the friends I was teaching there.

And that I, a stay at home writer, would get new cats in 2019, after my apartment had been renovated.

I didn't know when I would start making a living selling books, but I did know I would have to let the studio go, if it took too long.

Which is why there was an alternative plan.

OPTION 2.

WRITE, SELL TOO FEW BOOKS, CANCEL YOGA STUDIO, DOWNSIZE LIFE TO MINIMUM INCOME LEVEL, GET A JOB AS A JANITOR, WORK 40 HOURS A WEEK,
WRITE AT NIGHT TO STAY SANE,
DON'T TAKE CATS,
LOSE SOCIAL LIFE, BECOME LONELY,
NO COMPLAINING BECAUSE SO MANY PEOPLE HAVE OBLIGATIONS NEXT TO THEIR 40 HOUR JOB

Two options! This was an actual plan!

And of course the second option was less attractive than the first, but surely no reason to get a heart attack right?

The persistent pain in my chest could also be caused by a hidden backup plan, working title:

UNDER THE BRIDGE WITH A BOTTLE OF RED WINE

In this third option, I had continued the yoga studio just a little too long, downsized insufficiently, or I had not managed to get a job as a janitor.
In that scenario I would end up homeless and with nothing to show for, writing in paper notebooks I carried with me, and with limited to no options to get any posts out into the world.
Maybe they would be released after I died, maybe not.

Still suffering from insomnia I realized I needed to prioritize self-care.
I bet William Dafoe slept great, and he wasn't making money from his yoga mat, either.
I was convinced that if I focused on doing my daily yoga practice, I too would be able to sleep, and I would stop suffering from pain in my chest.

But since it was a pretty ungodly hour for yoga, I decided to masturbate instead.
(!!)
So I went onto Twitter, to the TL of Steve Holmes.

Steve Holmes is my favorite porn actor, and unlike Facebook, Twitter lets you (and Steve) post EVERYTHING.
I don't have to download or Google or pay: I can get aroused just browsing the promotional gifs, trailers and clips on Steve Holmes' TL.

Between all the porn (enough to ensure I would have no trouble masturbating) I clicked to Paige Owens, one of the actresses Steve had worked with.

And I found this tweet from her:

If being a hoe has taught me anything in this life,

it's that all of your pain can be turned into pleasure.

Paige Owens (18+) on Twitter

And I stopped. Of course! She was right! This was my specialty, this was what I was all about.
And why, although I had not heard from my lover Mr.Big for a while, I liked him not contacting me as much as I liked it if he did.

The pain of loneliness made the pleasure of seeing him, so much sweeter.
Just like sex, where pain makes the pleasure more intense. I knew I had the same fetish in life as well, but I had not realized until Paige's tweet that I needed this.

That I would rather suffer heart pains at night, than to live a balanced life.
I didn't need sales posts and a steady income selling books.
I didn't need a two hour yoga practice.
For me as a writer, a submissive, a pain junkie;
I needed that pain in my chest as much as I needed tough love from Mr.Big.

I closed Twitter, masturbated, and slept like a baby.

Turning pain into pleasure
was written on 22 July 2018

10
WHITE HEAT

Erotica writer by day, yoga teacher by night;
That's how LS Harteveld has lived her life for over a decade.
Which was all fine until she stopped being a yoga teacher and now
two parts of her personality are at each other's throats.

You don't decide to end a fifteen year career as a yoga teacher overnight.
I had actually already made the decision last summer, but turned it back when I realized I needed the studio address, due to Dutch legislation.
Unless I looked forward to having my home address being made public by the Chamber of Commerce.

Eh... public address, while writing hot stories about my sex life?
Unacceptable.
Dutch legislation is pretty strict.
Writers too, have to register as entrepreneurs.

So I decided to stay on as a yoga teacher. That way I could make the money back on my business location. The only thing I changed was I switched from teaching group classes to privates.
And I was doing okay.
Or maybe I just didn't really think about it and had made a pragmatic decision.

But last Wednesday I ran into a colleague and she asked how I was doing.

"I don't know really. I just realized my calendar is empty. I don't have any appointments anymore."

I could still give it an extra push and use the upcoming months to make my new business work. But if I would stop now I wouldn't have to inform or disappoint anybody.
I could just sneak out.

There had already been enough drama and goodbyes when I had ended my group classes. And now after the initial bookings my calendar was open...
I was free.
"I have no idea how I feel about this," I said to my colleague.
But it was clear that the lack of clients wasn't exactly crushing me.

And indeed, within a day after the conversation with my colleague, I made the decision to quit and this time for good. I was pretty relieved, maybe a bit numb.
Until the truth kicked in and I fell into a crisis.

It was as if every part of my personality had to be taken down before I could be rebuild.
After a few days I woke up still feeling sore, and with the same violent headache that had put me to sleep. But before I got up, I saw a vision.
Who I was supposed to be.
How I was supposed to look.
And what I was supposed to do.
The headache disappeared and I felt reborn.

From now on I would be a fulltime writer.
Which was honestly just a formality, a choice to call it by its name because I had been writing erotica and diaries under pen name LS Harteveld for over a decade.
And I had six years of writing for my studio, under my belt.

Writing had already been a fulltime job and every time I had been in the middle of a writing spree and had to go to the studio, I had felt where my loyalty lay.

And what could easily be suspended.

But from now on it was official, and I really was a writer.

I was going to keep writing under both names, both accounts.

Which was funny because up until now I had always assumed LS Harteveld had been my "real" writing. That the other stuff, under my real name, was just to position myself and sell the yoga classes. But I now realized that I liked that work too.

I could curate that, and create it into books, and make it even better by including some extra posts from LS Harteveld!

For example my pieces on Star Wars, Madonna or pop culture. There was no reason to have a pen name or be secretive about those.

I looked forward to positioning myself as a rebel yoga teacher, under my real name. Who after fifteen years was going to share what she really thought.

And suddenly I was thinking along a line that was making LS Harteveld territorial. I could hear her growling every time I added a topic or a blogpost of hers that would look pretty neat in my rebel yoga teacher book.

But it wasn't until I was considering including my pieces on Steve Holmes and pornography, that I felt I was crossing a line.

I was breaking the agreement that LS Harteveld would have the diaries, and sexually explicit content. Therefor I could not call my debut book under my real name:

How I was enlightened by Madonna, Kylo Ren and pornography.

Before I could consider how I would actually feel about discussing double penetration on national TV, that last word (pornography) would already have LS Harteveld stepping in.
"Sex is ME. Porn is MY PART!"

No matter how famous I would be, under my real name, it would always be the toned down version of me. The side everyone, from the mailman to the exes from a hundred years ago, could Google. A highly productive side, who had her own blog, published rebel yoga books, and was a true power woman.

But like Yin and Yang, it would still be just the light half.
Holding only a little spot of darkness.
And everybody would be all like:
"Oh wow! She's showing her dark side. How brave!"

Not knowing that the real darkness, including Steve Holmes, pornography, and double penetration, were all kept somewhere else.
Like treasures.
Safely stored, on the dark side.

White Heat
was written on 8 October 2018

11
HANKY PANKY

Even though Lauren's no longer crying on a daily basis, that doesn't mean she's her old self.
Yet.

When I was stressed out, I was aware that I wasn't masturbating. I lost all touch with my physical body.
I didn't even dress the way I normally do. Hoodies and comfortable pants seemed to be naturally drawn to my sadness.
I was wearing them without making a conscious choice to do so.

And although the problem was obviously on a way more existential level, I kept thinking:
"If only I could masturbate! Everything would be alright!"
I sometimes even went as far as to browse Steve Holmes' timeline on Twitter, which is my go-to if I don't bother to turn myself on with thoughts.
One quick look of my favorite porn star doing his thing is enough. Or it should be.
Except that it hadn't been for nearly two weeks.

That's when you know you have issues. And I already knew that. I was hoping masturbation would give me a hard reset and snap me out of it.

Yesterday I was still not functioning sexually, despite having solved my problem. I suggested to my creativity coach to include this into our call.
Where's my lust?

That was around midnight, writing that email. And just putting it in writing, giving it a place, was apparently the incentive it needed. I went to bed, masturbated, had merely four hours sleep before I had to get up, and I was fine all day.

This doesn't mean it is where I want it to be.

I can't imagine having real sex. Or doing yoga or cycling, other than a simple commute.

Every confrontation with my body, like waxing my legs, still feels completely off. Even putting on my clothes! As if I'm dressing a slightly overweight doll.

Still, real sex is actually the easiest way for me reconnect. To feel that lovely bigger body of mine is really made for it.

Rough sex.

Eye staring melt-together sex.

Role playing oh-my-God-not-there sex.

We cherish a whole bucket list of fantasies I still want to play out. Like a perverted treasure.

With all the other forms of physical activity, satisfaction is not guaranteed. And like I said, even masturbation cannot be done on command.

But when I see my lover Mr.Big, and we don't have sex?

It's more out of insecurity because I didn't shave my pubes or didn't shower right before. Or because it's not practical.

I can't remember ever saying no because I wasn't aroused.

I always want him when I see him.

He is, what makes me tick.

Hanky Panky
was written on 27 November 2018

12
SEX TALK

Like all philosophers, his job wasn't to be a philosopher.
And in his case it was an obvious one:
He was an artist.
Someone who creates exactly what he wants and manages to get paid for it. Or takes a temp job to make ends meet.

I've always considered myself an artist too.
Initially I called myself a writer, but since I have no interest in the craft itself nor in other writers unless they write novels based on their own lives, it soon became apparent I wasn't a writer at all.
I am a thinker.

I want to know the meaning behind a situation, a feeling, a moral judgement. I just keep on poking and unraveling until I know Why it is so.
And from there I will change reality, by redefining it through writing.

You can say the writing is my art, but in reality the process of taking everything in, digesting it, and creating new ideas about it, is my art.
My art starts when I open my eyes in the morning, and start to think about something.
I usually don't leave the bed, until I have so much to say about the topic, I can't think any more without first releasing it onto the page.

Maybe between the philosopher and me, I was actually more of a philosopher than he was. But regardless of who was what, we turned out to be extremely compatible.

So compatible that I told him all my sex secrets from the last four years, which I had not told anyone in a long time. The friends I could discuss this with, had already heard all these stories, and my secret lover Mr.Big and me had not had that kind of groundbreaking sex in a long time.

I had nothing new to tell.

But the philosopher didn't know me, and he met my non-negotiable criteria to sharing my sex stories.

These criteria were:

1. that someone was male

2. that he was sexually active and preferably pretty entrepreneurial with the whole thing, and

3. that he had a complete understanding that sharing my sex secrets – which were not really secrets at all, I just chose not to share – but he needed to understand that me sharing my sex secrets didn't mean that we were going to have sex.

That I was sharing them for my own pleasure, to relive the moment.

Late last year, I decided the only thing I am actively going to nurture is the sexual relationship I have with myself. I'm going to break the almost junkie-dealer dependency I have created with my supplier Mr.Big. Talking about my sex life, is like creating a glow of years past, to warm myself by.

More than ever, I wanted to tell about the times when I did still have an exciting sex life. And had cycled home with violent cramps in my pelvic floor, when my body was throwing a tantrum after anal sex. Times that belonged to the past.

Maybe it had been bad timing, in 2018. Maybe our dates had been on the wrong days, when I wasn't ready either physically or mentally.

Sometimes I thought we didn't have that same foundation anymore, of trust, and surrender. That the foundation where I trusted my body to him, and he trusted his whole life to me, was gone.

In the heyday, he had owned my body. Not in the master-slave way, at least not explicitly. But he had been sexually dominant. He didn't ask or hesitate, the way other men had. Instead he would seduce me into full submission, until I was begging for it.

And if I was lucky, we would uplevel our game to where he didn't ask at all, and just took me, abused me, raped me.
He had been the only man, with whom I didn't have to play-act really poorly, in order to make sure he wouldn't feel like he was doing something wrong.

I would fight back and cry real tears, and the pleasure was unbelievable. Yet at the same time, he knew when to stop before I did. Before I had decided if I was still up for this, he'd stop and ask:
"Are you okay?"
He knew me better than I knew myself.

And yet 2018 had gone by without being on that edge with him. I would receive minimal but sweet messages, an occasional platonic date, and satisfying but rather toned down sex compared to what we used to have.
And because I wanted to know Why, I came up with a reason.

The reason we stopped having that type of sex, is because something has shifted between us. And it's not "lust turns into love", which is the most probable cause, when you've been "together" for four years.

In our case it's because our relationship isn't stable anymore. From the outside it still looks like a regular mistress and lover relationship, but I fell in love with someone else for the first time.

And around that same time I felt something shift on his side as well.
Maybe there is someone else, I don't know.
But I suspect we don't have that same level of trust, where he trusts
me with his life/his integrity/his secret.
And in return I can trust him with my body.

I hope 2019 is going to be different. But if it's not that's okay too.
I've internalized my entire sexuality, and let go of the need to make
things work in the outside world. I am my own woman now.

Which was why talking to the philosopher about my sex life, was more
than welcome. The philosopher had past all three tests.
The first one: He was male.
The second one: He had an adventurous sex life.
He flaunted a "don't know which side is up" approach to sex, that had
of course resulted in the most messy sex life since Kurt Cobain and
Courtney Love.
Perfect.
I will never talk about my sex life with men who are not happy with
theirs or who are married.

I have one married friend, the Archaeologist, with whom I did talk
about my sex life on two occasions. The first occasion was when I had
anal sex with Mr.Big for the first time. A story I somehow managed to
stretch for an hour!
And the first time I told it (to my friend Pierre) it had been three hours.
An hour was the condensed version. I have no idea how!
Losing my anal virginity is the opening story from my book Big.
How are you going to fill three hours with what's written on a few
pages?

The second time I talked to the married Archaeologist about my sex
life, was when Mr.Big had used three butt plugs on me, ranging from
the size of a thin penis, to the size of a really thick one.

It was not just my achievement, that it fit:
Mr.Big had been extremely gentle.

I'm starting to believe that Mr.Big understands the art of balancing:
Whenever he can feel I am tensed about something, for example the
first time I was in his apartment, he downplays himself completely.
And upon seeing that largest butt plug anyone would feel intimidated.
Afterwards I sent the picture of the three butt plugs to my gay best
friend, and even he was intimidated!

So when something is already stressful, or exciting to me, Mr.Big is
extra gentle and sweet.
Which can also explain why we didn't do anything sexually remarkable
in 2018. Our affair was going through hard times, and we don't
communicate about such things.
The stress levels just build up.
The power play we used to have dates back to 2017 and before that;
When the situation on all other levels, was completely stable.

I could never have a messy sex life, the way the Philosopher had. I need
a clearly defined relationship, like the one from a mistress and her
lover, so I can play and experiment sexually.

The Philosopher also met the third criteria:
He understood that me talking about sex, didn't mean that we were
going to have sex.
Although this was obviously the hardest one.
But I took my chances because I was excited to share so I talked about
anal sex, butt plugs, power play.

And he wanted to know which role I had during power play (this was
at the beginning of our conversation) and he managed to guess wrong.
And even to back it up with completely invalid arguments, on why he
thought that.

I liked that. He wasn't afraid to be wrong, just as he wasn't afraid to be rejected.

He made me realize that's why "normal" men bore me:
They communicate in a way so that I can't reject them.

Just yesterday someone who has been trying to get my attention for years, opened his car window to talk to me, again skillfully ignoring my cold shoulder responses. And then said: "If you want to, come over, right?"

Like a sales man he's aware that I'll jump at the first opportunity to say No. All men do. That's why they never ask you something you can say No to, like asking you out.

Another reason why they don't ask you out, is that they're married and they don't want to go out. But I never invest in chatting on Whatsapp or something.
Either we see each other in real life, or we don't see each other at all. Period.
And not asking me out because of fear of rejection, but in the meantime waving your neediness in my face, signaling "Pick me! Pick me!", has to be one of the things that makes women resort to violence.

The Philosopher on the other hand, was an entirely different cattle of fish.
Just like he had not been shy at all, about asking me out on a date.

He was now shameless in his analysis on why I was dominant in bed. I think his strongest argument was that I was obviously ballsy and strong, so I could never be on the Anastacia Steele end of the stick.

Anastacia Steele is the submissive virgin from 50 Shades of Grey. 50 Shades was actually the Philosopher's main source of information in order to determine whether I was dominant or submissive. Again, something normal men would try to hide.

They'd say: "Well I had this woman once and based on that, my estimate is..."

The Philosopher was wrong, but he wasn't afraid to be wrong nor was he afraid to flaunt his limited knowledge on the matter and his sketchy sources.

I loved it.

So naturally I informed him that I was submissive, and had been for as long as I could remember.

He also asked me why I liked anal sex. From a woman's perspective he couldn't see the benefit.

This time – something that spoke for him – he indicated that he was curious. But that I should only answer if I wanted to.

I wanted to.

I answered the reason I liked anal sex was not a physical one: it was entirely mental. It fit in with being submissive. It was on that fine line between pleasure and pain, between surrender and humiliation. It was an absolute mindfuck.

As was my entire sex life.

I explained that I was not into things like massages, multiple orgasms, or anything physical. The whole thing, my entire sexuality, was a mind game.

And he asked me about porn. Which he assumed I wouldn't like then, because it was entirely physical.

"On the contrary!" I answered.

And I explained to him mainstream porn had so many rough, degrading sex, I could watch any porn clip on my Twitter feed to get satisfied.

And that I was probably Steve Holmes (a porn star) biggest fan.

The Philosopher only interrupted my praise of porn, to ask me if I was a real person.

We ordered our too-many-to-count drink. The only time I remember drinking this much was on my nights with the Archaeologist.
When I had told the Archaeologist the story about the butt plugs, I remembered I still had the picture of the toys on my phone.
The one I had sent to my gay best friend.
"I have a picture!" I had exclaimed.
A photo of the three black butt plugs, medium to extra large, standing in the windowsill. Just like my gay best friend, the Archaeologist could not believe the largest one had actually gone in.

I told the Philosopher that when the Archaeologist and me had said our goodbyes, he had turned around, in the middle of the street.
Staring at me, as if he was in trance.
"I still can't believe it," was the only thing he said.

In the middle of the night the Philosopher and me said our goodbyes, in a warm hug, that was not sexual and I didn't want it to be either.
But I just had the best day in years.
Part of me wanted something, I just didn't know what it was.
"I still can't believe it," The Philosopher whispered softly.
Neither could I.

Sex talk
was written on 3 January 2019

13
VEGETARIAN PORN

About two weeks ago I saw a simple but totally hot porn clip. It was on Twitter, and it featured a tattooed guy and a petite brunette.

That was all I had to go on.

I didn't search "rapey sex" on Twitter, because I do not want to think about what shows up if you do that.

And it wasn't of any use to check the timelines of the porn actors I follow either.

First of all because there are so many. And secondly, because as I recall this clip was not posted by someone I follow.

And I didn't even "like" the tweet with the clip.

Liking is a way of showing appreciation, but it also archives the tweet to a list with "liked" tweets.

And this not-liking was now costing me dearly, because otherwise I could have browsed my "liked tweets" list, and I would not have to go on a seemingly impossible search trying to retrieve it.

But I never "like" (mark with a heart) porn clips on Twitter, because they then show up in the TLs of people who follow you.

Your follower also get recommendations, based on who you follow, but to me that's a different story.

I think it's funny and slightly rebellious, that my followers see recommendations such as:

"LS Harteveld follows" over a tweet with double penetration.

Yet I'm either too shy, too suave, or maybe too much of a flat-out liar to actually like such a tweet.

Well worse!

Way worse!

I do *like* it, as in the feelings I have towards it!

But then I don't reward the video with a like-heart, because I don't want people to see I watched it.

And this weekend that cowardice behavior came back with a vengeance!

Because I was still thinking about the clip, masturbated to it and everything.

I was getting slightly panicky at the thought of how difficult it was going to be to find it back.

In the unlikely event you think you can help me, here are the specs:

– video about two people fucking, in a bed, poorly lit.
Missionary with petite long-haired brunette and a big tattooed guy on top covering her mouth with his hand.

It was this feature with the hand, that gave the video it's fascinating rapey, non-consensual, appeal. The reason I'm still determined to mine through Twitter until I find it.

– length: 1 minute or so

– visual: black and white/ or very dark. As if "the abuse" takes place at night, and is shot by a clandestine camera.

In the clip, the man gets off of her and she sits up. They're probably going to change position, and the camera sways more towards the end of the bed.

And there were other signs too, that it was regular porn and not something creepy. For example, he doesn't cover her mouth for "real", just occasionally.

That's the description of the clip I have been searching for.
So far I've spent six hours total I think, trying to retrieve it.

I started with the Twitter account of one brunette porn star, going through her TL until Christmas last year, and I would note down Twitter names of other female actors who fit the profile and of tattooed actors I saw in the videos.
With some accounts it took me half an hour, to browse back for one month.

I don't have my computer at home, due to a set of boring circumstances, so I had to do it on my phone.
Up to half an hour per actor, and clicking any clip that didn't provide a screenshot (so I couldn't identify what it was).

Saturday night I went to sleep feeling totally wasted from four hours of porn browsing on my phone. I felt like that princess from Rumpelstiltskin where she gets impossible sorting assignments.
If evil Rumpelstiltskin had offered to help me out, I would have taken it.

I went to sleep and had a dream so heartbreaking and awful, I woke up a vegetarian.
And I think it had to do with the timeline from the last porn star I had been browsing: A buff tattooed male vegan actor, who tweeted about animal rights in between porn videos.
I did not even watch the animal rights things, but apparently I didn't even have to, in order to be sent off on a guilt-trip dream.

So the story now is that porn made me a vegetarian.
Which is a good story.
And I've decided I will write about what I dreamed.

So if you don't want to read it, just like I didn't want to watch or read the animal rights tweets in the actor's timeline, then just skip to the next paragraph.

(...)

Okay, so the dream that made me a vegetarian was this:

I was in the meat department of a very fancy supermarket, or it was a huge buffet with refrigerated sections.
On one plate a baby donkey the size of a rabbit was lying on ice, but it was still alive/ breathing.
Which was of course horrible.

But while I was still trying to get my head around to what I was seeing here, I noticed another donkey on a silver platter.
It was the height of a Jack Russell, maybe slightly smaller, and it was trying to get up onto its hooves.
The slippery surface of the silver platter nearly made that impossible, but it kept on trying.

Ultimately the miniature donkey succeeded, and walked off.
Straight to the foal on the ice. It pulled it off, and started licking it to life, but the baby donkey had stopped breathing.

I woke up and decided I would never eat meat again.

Vegetarian Porn
was written on 28 January 2019

14
A NIGHT AS VALUABLE AS ALL OTHERS

In December I decided I would evacuate my house, during the current three week period of indoor renovation.

I was going to get a whole house all to myself. That was Plan A.

The problem with this, aside from the costs, was that all holiday cabins were located outside of the city, and I don't have a car.

Plan B was to get a hotel, downtown.

Where I would feel uplifted by the inner-city buzz and could easily meet with friends. But the downside was that a hotel didn't offer my own facilities to cook or do laundry.

Plan C would have been to live with my mother, if it wasn't for the fact that I had discarded that one.

I had just started my new career as a writer, publisher, speaker. And under a new name, LS Harteveld. Living with my mother was simply not an option for two reasons.

The first was that staying over with someone is too close to becoming homeless. As a beginning entrepreneur, I did't want to think about how much or how little it would take to end up that way. Sleeping over at friends or my mother felt like I had one foot in being homeless.

The second reason sleeping with my mother was not a good idea, was because I needed to get into this role, this new identity of LS Harteveld.

My mother is one of the people who will never see me as LS Harteveld, and that is cool. But I can't build up LSH and at the same time be confronted with my old, broken identity.

With the woman who is completely drained after being a yoga teacher for 15 years, and who doesn't want to work another day in her life.

Also sexually, sleeping over at my mother's would be a disaster.

Although I was of course also sexual under my old name, having my own space, my own identity, my own energy when I go to bed and may or may not masturbate, are all key to my sense of self.

Going to bed every night feeling like a child would be killing for any career.

But for someone who has decided that she wants to feel sexual and fuckable 24/7, it is particularly demotivating.

I've long considered it strange that on one hand I decided I would internalize my sexuality – and I did. If my lover Mr.Big would stop seeing me, it would not influence how I see myself, nor spark the serial dater in me.

And on the other hand I go through lengths to always have my own space, and to only BE in places that uplift me.

That hold some kind of sexual or inspirational energy.

At first glance it didn't make sense

Until I realized that OF COURSE it made sense!

The reason I have been able to internalize my sexuality, and become independent of Mr.Big or other men I might fall in love with and would be open to dating, is because I am so terribly picky about where and with whom I spend my time.

My surroundings mirror a successful, sexual, independent woman.

That is why I can keep that vision alive of being LS Harteveld.

If I would live for three weeks without a sewer, a bathroom, heating, or kitchen, and camp in my living room with an electric heater, an electric cooker and a chemical toilet;

I would betray her.

LS Harteveld would never settle for that. It would be impossible to develop myself and crush my new career under those circumstances.

So, that had been my decision making process weeks ago.

And in the end the Universe helped me to get it all done without spending any money. Thanks to two medical diagnosis, I was given the keys a temporary home.

It was all last minute, and this home too, had some renovations planned, during that period. But that wasn't the worst.

I also had a cut internet cable, which was discovered under the pavement after four days of not having Wifi and countless calls to the provider.

I had a malfunctioning central heating, which combined with radiators being taken down temporarily for the renovations, led to ten days of dysfunctional heaters.

When all those things were finally fixed my happiness was immediately restored.

It was a relief to notice just how much energy and frustration had been directly linked to having workers and mechanics and malfunctioning everything.

But now it was all up, and for the remainder of my time I could live in my new apartment and sleep in a wonderful bed.

I even fantasized what it would be like, if my lover would come over, and play out my new consent fantasy.

It was a video from Twitter with a petite brunette being fucked by a buff tattooed guy.
The lighting was poor, it was dark, and it was as if she was raped in her own bed.
Now I'll say it again: I didn't for one minute believe this was real. It was just nice non-consensual-play porn.
Which made me terribly hot.

And being in this bed I didn't know, in a house that was foreign to me, was the perfect spot for me to play this out.
I was hoping my lover would be able to make it, before I would go back to my own apartment.
And now that everything was up and running, I could make that happen.
Or so I thought.

Because you know what happened yesterday?

At 7.30 AM there was an asbestos renovation of the toilet, which the building cooperation had forgot to mention. But worse than that:

When I got back at 10 PM, totally wasted after a super-long day behind my desk, trying to get my work done, the toilet was not properly installed. It flooded straight into holes leading to the apartment downstairs.

Good thing I peed only a tiny little bit!

I spent an hour making phone calls to the building cooperation, and talking to the downstairs neighbor on what to do, now that his apartment was flooding for the second time that day.

Around midnight I arrived back at my mother's, who had made me a bed, for which I was so grateful.

I'm now going home to see if they have everything installed again. And if they haven't I'm taking a hotel.

I already know which one; I've been curious about it for a long time!

Because I'm not spending another night at my mother's.

I once read this story about two sisters who went on a holiday, and checked into a hotel that was far more basic, than they had anticipated.

One sister didn't make a fuss about it.

But the other one insisted they'd find a better hotel.

Because this night was just as important as all others.

And it is.

A night as valuable as all others
was written on 31 January 2019

Post-scripts:

For
3. And AWAY Is Avery.
How a disappearing escort became my muse

Avery Moore has picked up her work under this name.
If you Google "Avery Moore escort" you should be able to find her
website, Instagram and Twitter.

For
13. Vegetarian Porn

A few weeks after writing *Vegetarian Porn*, I found the clip.

It was a preview to a video called "A Quiet Fuck"
and the name of the actress is Avery Moon

ABOUT THIS BOOK
A PORN STAR LOVE LIFE

I didn't plan on making this book, not on bundling up all my blog posts about my life-long fascination with pornography and sex work.
And yet now that it's done it makes so much sense, and I would not have wanted it any other way.
Of course this is a book that deserves to be in print!

Very few women like me, speak up about liking pornography in pretty much the same way men like it.
This book gives us, and that includes myself, a voice.
But there is something bigger at stake here.

Because sex work is still not treated equally to other work.
Not even in the most liberal of countries.

Whereas most of us would agree the majority of labor is transactional, seldom intrinsically motivated (and when it is, you're usually taken advantage of and paid far beneath your market value);
That all work either entails physical or mental health risks, and that burnout has become pandemic;
That many of the mid-level jobs qualify as bullshit jobs, where no one benefits, and that are devastating to our sense of self-esteem and sense of purpose.
Despite all of those things?
Sex work is never treated as the rest of the service industry, and in film and show business it is not treated like the rest of the entertainment industry.

Even though sex work and porn pay significantly better than average, offer autonomy, a flexible work schedule, and they are a great equalizer since no diplomas are required to start and if all legal barriers were taken away, there would be ample opportunities for entrepreneurship.

It is also the only line of work where women have a competitive advantage and are generally paid more than men.

It would be vanity to think that this book can change the marginalized position of working in the sex industry or as a sex worker.

These are merely my own diary entries and stories related to the moments I enjoyed pornography, or was inspired by sex workers. I was merely a consumer, a bystander, someone on Twitter.

But now that I am writing the parting words for this book, I can see that the least I can do, is not *not* talk about it.

And share the stories I have written and identify myself as sex-work positive, as one sex worker called it.

And as porn-positive.

And so it is.

Lauren Harteveld
12 September 2021

All books available worldwide at:

https://www.lulu.com/spotlight/LaurenandLulu

The best book to buy after *A Porn Star Love Life*, is

Big
diaries and erotica (2015-2016)

Mr.Big and me watched pornography together, and our sex life was
heavily influenced by shared fantasies and pornographic imagery

THE WAIT WORTH 8

All released in 2017

1. **Mango**, een novelle *Dutch*
   Seksuele safari, van de jaren '80 tot de zero's.

2. **Dutch American Diary** (2008-2009)
   Lauren is in love with two men;
   One cunning wizard and one half her age.
   ~Dutch American Diary part 1

3. **22 Erotische Verhalen** *Dutch*
   Literaire pornografie in de geest van Anais Nin
   en Isabel Allende.

4. **LS Diary** (2012-2013)
   About three dark men and Lauren getting naked on stage.
   Not necessarily together.
   ~Dutch American Diary part 2

5. **De Candystop** (2013) *Dutch*
   Waar de Nederlandse literatuur tot stilstand komt door een
   Marokkaanse lekkernij.

6. **Bedtime Stories** (2014)
   Facing her demons and her muse, Lauren's sexual history
   gets its worthy finale.
   ~Dutch American Diary part 3

7. **Mirage** (2014)
   Giving you a little dessert, with all gorgeous writers from
   previous books.
   ~Dutch American Diary epilogue

8. **Big**, diaries and erotica (2015-2016)
   The crown to Lauren's life; a secret affair with her Biggie.

SEPARATE BOOKS

These books are not part of the numbered (diary) series

- **Het Boek Benjamin** *Dutch and English*
  Collected works, contains book 1 -8 from the previous page

- **Witte Tijgerin**, *Dutch*
  Gids voor solitaire vrouwen die een geweldig seksleven willen en plenty energie.

- **The White Tigress Yoga Workbook**

- **The Mistress Speaks** (2018 - 2021)
  Channeling a lost archetype

- **The Beach, C.** (2018 - 2021)
  Diary, letters and essays inspired by Basic Instinct's Catherine Tramell

- **Star Wars is finally telling women *cross out* everybody to start enjoying The Thing** (2018 - 2019)
  And other deeply personal blogposts about the sequel trilogy that did not age well

- **A Porn Star Love Life** (2015 - 2019)
  stories that brush on, toy with and praise, my love for pornography and sex workers